THE SUN BEAR

Do Your Kids Know This?

A Children's Picture Book
Amazing Creature Series

Tanya Turner

PUBLISHED BY:

Tanya Turner

Copyright © 2016

TABLE OF CONTENTS

The Sun Bear 5

Getting to Know the Sun Bear 7

Habitat 12

How Do Sun Bears Behave? 14

Diet 17

Breeding and Reproduction 20

Population Status 23

Threats 25

Sun Bears and Humans 26

The Sun Bear

The Sun Bear.
Image from Shutterstock by Molly Marshall.

The Sun Bear – which is also called Malayan Sun Bear, Honey Bear, and Dog Bear, is indeed a species of bear. It is sometimes called Honey Bear since it likes eating honey so much.

But why is it also called Dog Bear? If you take a good look at it, you will realize that it somewhat looks like a dog. In fact, even its size can be compared to a dog since it is not as big as other species of bears.

This type of bear is really unique. In fact, it is not like other species of bears. However, one thing is for sure – it is just as loveable as other types of bears.

The Sun Bear is a small species of bear.
Image from Shutterstock by BENZINE.

Getting to Know the Sun Bear

The Sun Bear is one of the smallest species of bears. It only measures about 47 to 59 inches in length, so its size can be compared to a big dog.

The male Sun Bears are usually bigger than the females. Even still, they are not as big as the really big bears we see in movies and in zoos. Although they only weigh about 325 grams at birth, their weight can reach anywhere from 60 to 176 pounds.

It's quite easy to recognize a Sun Bear – you just need to know their general physical appearance and color. In the case of this type of bear, they have short fur or coat (or hair). Although most of them are black, their color can also have some variety. There are Sun Bears, for example, that are reddish brown in color, and there are also those that are grayish.

It's important to know that Sun Bears have patches on their chests, too. This patch (or mark) is unique in every individual bear, so it can also serve as their identifying mark. If two Sun Bears look very much alike, you can look at their chest patch and identify them from this.

Aside from having unique looking patches on their chests, these can also vary in color. Sun Bears can have white, yellow or orange patches – and some of these patches can even have spots.

Sun Bears have dog-like qualities.

Image from Shutterstock by Artush.

Sun Bears also have dog-like qualities. Firstly, their snouts are short and broad. Secondly, they have big, fleshy heads that can have wrinkled skin (like some breeds of dogs).

A Sun Bear eating food.
Image from Shutterstock by Celso Diniz.

Their faces don't have a dark color, but are light-colored instead. As for their ears, they are small and rounded.

Another special quality of the Sun Bear is that it has a very long tongue that measures about eight to ten inches long. That's really long – in fact, Sun Bears have the longest tongue among all other bear species.

As with other types of bears, Sun Bears also have large teeth. They have strong jaws too, which they use to crush and chew their food.

A sleepy Sun Bear.
Image from Shutterstock by dibrova.

They also have noticeably large feet. In fact, when you look at the overall appearance of a Sun Bear, you will notice that its feet are quite large compared to its body.

The feet of Sun Bears are not structured to be aligned with their bodies. Instead, they are slightly turned inwards. Also, this type of bear has very large paws. As for their claws, these are curvy and long.

Don't think that the Sun Bear is an odd-looking creature because of its feet. As with other species of animals, everything and every part of this animal have their purposes. In this particular case, you will realize that this type of bear is capable of climbing trees. The ability to climb trees is a great skill because they will be able to escape their predators by doing this. Such a skill also provides the bear with more sources of food since they don't just have to rely on food that is found on the ground.

A Sun Bear in its natural habitat.
Image from Shutterstock by BENZINE.

Habitat

Most of the population (the remaining population, that is) of Sun Bears can be found in Southeast Asia. They are particularly found in the forests of India, Thailand, Burma, Borneo, Laos, Vietnam, Cambodia, and Sumatra.

Sun Bears used to live in the forest areas of Southern China, Tibet, and Bangladesh. However, this type of bear is now considered to be extinct in such places. Therefore, they are not totally extinct in the world but are only extinct in some of their original habitats.

For the places that still have Sun Bears – they can be found in areas with lots of trees and water sources. What's important to these bears for survival is food and water, of course, and they also need a place where they are not threatened. The forest is the best place for them since this is rarely visited by humans. Of course, there are predators around, but animals are used to fighting for their survival against other species of animals.

The Sun Bear has a really long tongue.

Image from Shutterstock by Dane Jorgensen.

A sleeping Sun Bear.
Image from Shutterstock by Geoffrey Kuchera.

How Do Sun Bears Behave?

When in their natural habitat (such as in the forest), Sun Bears are usually active during the day time. They use the light of day to roam around the forest and look for food. However, when Sun Bears are kept in captivity, they try to avoid humans as much as possible. Because of this, Sun Bears can be more active at night than during the day. While that doesn't necessarily mean sleeping throughout the day, their activities can be quite limited because they are not comfortable being around humans. When night time comes and people are no longer around, they tend to roam more as they are more comfortable in their surroundings.

Unlike other types of bears, Sun Bears don't hibernate. Hibernation is more common for bears that live in cold places, but as you can see, these bears live in places with minimal cold months, so hibernating is not necessary.

As tree-dwelling bears, Sun Bears can quickly climb up trees. They work their way up the trees by holding on to branches and using their claws to securely grab on the branches of trees. For really big trees, Sun Bears can hug the trunk of the tree while climbing it.

Know that Sun Bears are not social animals. In fact, you will find them alone and by themselves most of the time. Unless it's breeding season – where you will usually see them in pairs (male and female).

In spite of being solitary creatures that prefer to be alone most of the time, they can tolerate the presence of other Sun Bears in their chosen area in the forest. For instance, if there are fruit bearing trees, you will often find a number of Sun Bears eating from the same tree without fighting.

Sun Bears can climb up on trees.
Image from Shutterstock by Don Fink.

Sun Bears are actually known to be friendly creatures. In fact, this is the reason why some people keep them as pets (like dogs). However, don't think that they are totally gentle because they are still wild animals – when startled and surprised, they can be quite aggressive. Don't forget either, they have big teeth and really sharp claws – you wouldn't want to make them angry at you and attack you.

A group of Sun Bears.
Image from Shutterstock by wannasak saetia.

Diet

Sun Bears are omnivores which means they eat both plants and meat from other animals. Their diet is comprised of different types of food as they have learned to adapt to the different situations in the wild. Food sources can be very limited in the forest if an animal is a picky eater, so in the case of Sun Bears, they can eat small types of animals like rodents, lizards, birds, and turtles.

This type of bear even eats insects. Their long tongues prove to be especially useful for insects as they can reach small holes with their tongues to get termites, worms, beetles, and ants.

Sun Bears love eating honey.
Image from Shutterstock by Ross Gordon Henry.

As their name suggests, they are also honey eaters (like Winnie the Pooh), and they also eat fruits that grow in different seasons in the forest all throughout the year.

There are different types of food available to the Sun Bear every day. This is a good thing so they won't go hungry or starve to death. In case there are some shortages of food, they will immediately grab the first opportunity they have to eat when food becomes available again.

Needless to say, not eating for several days can take its toll on the Sun Bear and they can lose their fat. However, they can recover from this quickly and regain their fat as soon as they start eating again. They will simply reserve their energy when they are not eating so they don't become weak when food sources are limited.

Sun Bears sometimes have wrinkled foreheads.
Image from Shutterstock by Dane Jorgensen.

Breeding and Reproduction

When it's breeding season, male and female Sun Bears get together to mate. During the courtship stage, the male and female will communicate with each other by hugging and fighting. It would seem that they're fighting, but they're actually just courting each other.

There is no particular time of the year for Sun Bears to mate. Most of the time, this will depend on the female's health status and weather. The female needs to have enough fat reserves in her body to carry a cub (a baby Sun Bear). The weather should also be good (not too hot and not too cold) when Sun Bears breed because this will increase the cub's chances for survival. Also, there should be available food for the bears to eat so they can remain healthy throughout the breeding season and up to the time the cubs are born.

It will take about three months for the female Sun Bear to give birth to her cubs. She will prepare for this by making a nest in the tops of trees. Their nests can be similar to a bird's nest (but bigger, of course) – so the Sun Bear will gather branches and twigs for this.

Sun Bears have long claws.
Image from Shutterstock by Ross Gordon Henry.

The mother Sun Bear will make sure that her nest is stable and sturdy. She can also decide to build her nest inside a tree hole to secure her cubs from the weather.

Sun Bears live in the forest.
Image from Shutterstock by Jakrit Jiraratwaro.

A pregnant female Sun Bear can give birth to one to three cubs – but usually, she will only have one. A baby cub will be hairless and defenseless when it's born, that's why it will be totally dependent on its mother for food and safety.

A Sun Bear cub will actually stay with its mother up to adulthood. At about three months, it will start to run and play with other cubs. It will also go with its mother when traveling and looking for food – this will be its training period so that it can learn to survive on its own.

As cubs, baby Sun Bears will have loose skin on their necks. As you already know, they are quite vulnerable to attacks from predators since bigger animals will find them to be easy targets. By having loose skin on their necks, the cubs will be able to turn their heads when bitten on the back of their necks. This way, they can at least bite back or fight their enemies.

A young Sun Bear.
Image from Shutterstock by David Kucera.

Population Status

Sun Bears are currently Vulnerable to extinction. This means that we should be concerned about them because their population are no longer that high. Remember, some of the places they used to inhabit don't even have them anymore, and if their numbers continue to decrease, they can become endangered and extinct.

Being labeled Vulnerable is actually just one level below being labeled endangered. We don't want them to be endangered species because that will bring them closer to becoming extinct. All of them will be gone when they become extinct – and we don't want that.

A cute Sun Bear sticking its tongue out.
Image from Shutterstock by Vladimir Wrangel.

Threats

Habitat loss due to illegal logging is one of the biggest threats of animals living in forests. Because of the Sun Bear's nature, they can also be sold as pets.

As a species that is vulnerable to extinction, killing and catching Sun Bears is now illegal in a lot of countries.

A beautiful Sun Bear sitting alone.
Image from Shutterstock by Molly Marshall.

Sun Bears and Humans

Since Sun Bears are friendly creatures, some people keep them as pets. However, this is not a good idea because they are still wild animals and they will be happier when they are free in their natural habitat.

Disclaimer

The information contained in this book is for general information purposes only. The information is provided by the authors and, while we endeavor to keep the information up to date and correct, we make no representations or warranties of any kind, expressed or implied, about the completeness, accuracy, reliability, suitability or availability with respect to the book or the information, products, services, or related graphics contained in the book for any purpose. Any reliance you place on such information is therefore strictly at your own risk.

CPSIA information can be obtained at www.ICGtesting.com
Printed in the USA
LVIW01n1501120917
548428LV00011B/133